DISCOVER
Ocean Pollution

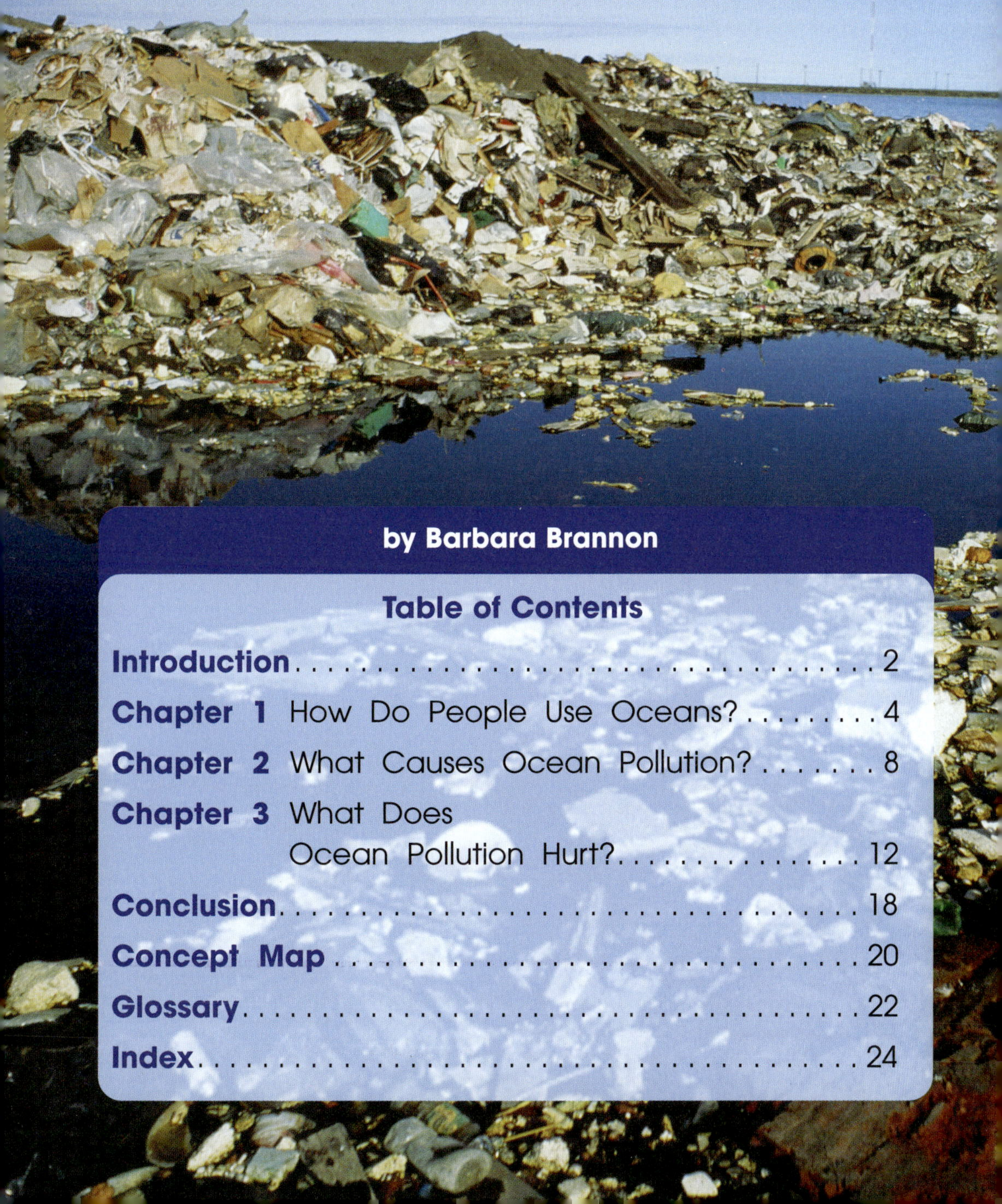

by Barbara Brannon

Table of Contents

Introduction	2
Chapter 1 How Do People Use Oceans?	4
Chapter 2 What Causes Ocean Pollution?	8
Chapter 3 What Does Ocean Pollution Hurt?	12
Conclusion	18
Concept Map	20
Glossary	22
Index	24

Introduction

People need **ocean plants**. People need ocean **animals**. People need ocean water. People need oceans.

Words to Know

 animals

 ocean

 people

 plants

 pollution

 salt

See the Glossary on page 22.

Chapter 1

How Do People Use Oceans?

People use oceans for food.

▲ People eat fish.

People use oceans for **salt**.

▲ People use salt.

It's A Fact
Oceans cover about $\frac{3}{4}$ of Earth.

People use oceans for oil.

▲ People use oil.

Chapter 1

People use oceans for sand.

▲ People use sand.

People use oceans for shells.

▲ People use shells.

How Do People Use Oceans?

People use oceans for fun.

▲ People use oceans.

Chapter 2

What Causes Ocean Pollution?

Chemicals cause ocean **pollution**.

It's A Fact
Chemicals in the air cause acid rain. Acid rain falls to Earth. Acid rain kills fish in the ocean.

▲ Chemicals cause pollution.

Gases cause ocean pollution.

▲ Gases cause pollution.

Chapter 2

Garbage causes ocean pollution.

▲ Garbage causes pollution.

Oil spills cause ocean pollution.

▲ Oil spills cause pollution.

What Causes Ocean Pollution?

People cause ocean pollution.

▲ People cause pollution.

Then and Now

People threw garbage in oceans. Now we have laws. We can not throw garbage in oceans.

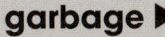 garbage ▶

Chapter 3

What Does Ocean Pollution Hurt?

Ocean pollution hurts fish.

It's A Fact

Lobsters are in danger. Lobsters live under rocks. Lobsters live on the ocean floor. Garbage is filling the homes of lobsters.

▲ Pollution hurts fish.

Chapter 3

Ocean pollution hurts sharks.

▲ Pollution hurts sharks.

Ocean pollution hurts whales.

▲ Pollution hurts whales.

What Does Ocean Pollution Hurt?

Ocean pollution hurts dolphins.

▲ Pollution hurts dolphins.

Ocean pollution hurts seals.

▲ Pollution hurts seals.

Chapter 3

Ocean pollution hurts plants.

▲ Pollution hurts plants.

What Does Ocean Pollution Hurt?

Ocean pollution hurts people.

▲ Pollution hurts people.

Conclusion

Ocean pollution hurts Earth.

Concept Map

Ocean Pollution

How Do People Use Oceans?

| food |
| salt |
| oil |
| sand |
| shells |
| fun |

What Causes Ocean Pollution?

| chemicals |
| gases |
| garbage |
| oil spills |
| people |

What Does Ocean Pollution Hurt?

- fish
- sharks
- whales
- dolphins
- seals
- plants
- people

Glossary

animals living things that can move around

*Ocean pollution hurts **animals**.*

ocean a large body of salt water

***Ocean** pollution hurts Earth.*

people human beings

***People** cause ocean pollution.*

plants living things that can not move around

*Ocean pollution hurts **plants**.*

pollution causing something to be soiled or harmed

*Ocean **pollution** hurts seals.*

salt white solid used on food

*People need oceans for **salt**.*

Index

animals, 2

chemicals, 8, 20

dolphins, 15, 21

Earth, 18

fish, 4, 12, 20

food, 4, 20

fun, 7, 20

gases, 9, 20

ocean, 2, 4-12, 14-18, 20-21

oil, 5, 10, 20

oil spills, 10, 20

people, 2, 4-7, 11, 17, 20-21

plants, 2, 26, 21

pollution, 8-18, 20-21

salt, 5, 20

sand, 6, 20

seals, 15, 21

sharks, 14, 21

shells, 6, 20

whales, 14, 21